T0208340

26
Days
To
Practice
Peace

CONLEE RICKETTS

BALBOA.
PRESS
A DIVISION OF HAY HOUSE

Balboa Press books may be ordered through booksellers or by contacting:

Balboa Press
A Division of Hay House
1663 Liberty Drive
Bloomington, IN 47403
www.balboapress.com
1 (877) 407-4847

Print information available on the last page.

ISBN: 978-1-9822-3121-7 (sc)
ISBN: 978-1-9822-3120-0 (hc)
ISBN: 978-1-9822-3127-9 (e)

Library of Congress Control Number: 2019909691

Balboa Press rev. date: 07/12/2019

Contents

Dedication

For Skye, L is for Love

Preface

This book started as a random scribbling in my writing journal in 2013. I started to make an alphabetical list of words that I live my life by, or words that I call on when my life is in the toilet. I was curious. I wanted to know if there was a word for every letter. There was. Then I thought I could take my list, expand it somehow, and have a gift to give as a small road map from distraction to discovery.

There the list sat—A to Z, twenty-six beautifully hand-scripted words—for a year. Then a blogging challenge found its way into my world in 2014, motivating me to finally expand on the list I had created: the "Blogging from A to Z Challenge," twenty-six blogs in twenty-six days over the course of a month with weekends off. I scrambled around the house, digging into all my old journals and pieces of paper I had tucked away here and there, looking for that list. The number 26 nudged me to know it was time to find my alphabet! I successfully finished the challenge on time, meeting some wonderful bloggers along the way. It was the best way to get me writing and keep me focused. I recommend it to anyone who loves to write and scribble: http://www.a-to-zchallenge.com/.

Life began to get in the way of my writing, as it tends to do. A new job, new responsibilities, new stress, and I set my list and my essays aside once again. "A is for Accept" kept bugging me. Acceptance kept hitting me in the face over and over again as I faced all my new challenges, until I realized that this was the book I needed to publish. It has been years since I scribbled my twenty-six words, and each word is still a guiding force in my life.

I chose the title *26 Days to Practice Peace* because it *is* a practice, and it *takes* practice. I have learned that I can stick with anything for a day. For my daughter, it used to be remembering to not cuss for a day. My colorful vocabulary used to be her pet peeve, but now in her teenage years my potty mouth goes unnoticed. I can refrain from sugar for a day, or potato chips for a day, or even remember to be kind for a day. It is the act of stringing those days together where I need the practice. You will find my ability to self-edit my colorful language ebbs and flows, just like my eating habits. So each day is a new focus, a new piece of behavior or frame of mind to embrace. We are simply practicing.

You will need to choose your own strategy. Perhaps you read the letter of the day before getting out of bed. Maybe you will choose to put sticky notes all around you to remind you where to place your focus for the day. Every time you lose focus and then remember for a quick instant that you forgot, simply smile at yourself, and pick up where you left off. "Oh, yeah, today I accept," or, "Oh, yeah, today I'm being compassionate." Trust me, you will veer off track a lot, and that's okay. No one is watching, judging, or keeping score. You are not "in trouble."

Another option might be to read the next day's letter before going to bed. Write it on the bathroom mirror with dry-erase markers; take a selfie in the mirror with your word. Set it as the background on your phone. Whatever you need to do to plan your day with your word, I encourage you to do it. Remember, we can do just about anything for a single day.

It's my hope for each of you that as the days pass and you think about the stories or ideas that spring to mind each day, you begin to feel a bit lighter, smile more often, and handle the various crap that comes your way with more grace and ease. Yes, I know I used crap and grace in the same sentence, but this is life and living, and both crap and grace are here.

It is twenty-six days. Not even a whole month. If you can do anything for a single day, then this will be twenty-six single days that connect and create a shift in your life.

For me, I know that I need to practice peace, expect miracles, love myself more, and trust that everything is exactly as it should be in this exact moment. But that takes practice. My life is about baby steps and small doses of things I am able to accomplish *now*, not some grand day in the future when everything in my life is "perfect." That day doesn't come, and even if it did come, I wouldn't recognize it as such. I wouldn't be paying attention to it because I would probably be worrying about the future or stuck in the past. I have to take one day at a time because that's the only day I have.

Join me in these small moments, and in twenty-seven days, we can look back together over some pretty good days with good moments and good lessons learned. I am excited to hear about your experience!

Introduction

Read. Reflect. Resolve.

The goal is to commit to some small action for twenty-four hours twenty-six times. Before you dig in, I want to provide you with a tool if you like structure. If you don't like structure, your best bet is to dive right in and invent your own structure as you go along to help you read, reflect, and resolve.

Disclaimer: Resolving to "be better, do better" is a pain in the ass. You are forced to look in a mirror that reflects the things you need to work on about yourself but that you probably don't realize exist at all. How can you tell you've found something to work on? They might be your worst days or even the boring days believe it or not.

The desire to become a better friend, partner, teammate, coworker, ultimately a better person, lies in your ability to acknowledge room for improvement. Those areas are the things we don't really relish examining, but if change is what you want, then the most difficult things you face are the ones with the best opportunities for growth.

It will be important to stay balanced and recognize all the great things the mirror will show you too. This is why I created a checklist for you.

At this point, you haven't even begun your first day, and you may be wondering, *What the hell is she saying?*

Let me give you an example. My ninety-one-year-old father wanted to move an old sewing machine down to the basement. Here's what happened, Dad says to me, "When you get a chance, can you help me move your grandmother's sewing machine into the basement?"

"Sure. Let me swap out laundry loads first." I go to the basement and begin switching my loads. Out of the corner of my ear, I hear clunk, shuffle, clunk, clunk! My jaw clenches with each clunk and shuffle. The knowledge of what he is trying to do has my inner voice screaming, *Jeez, Dad! I said I would help. Give me one minute!* "Dad, Wait for me," I yell from the washer and dryer.

"I'm fine," he puffs.

Then I lose it a little bit. My frustration explodes with a, "Why didn't you wait for me? I said I would help! Just because I didn't hop right to it the moment you asked doesn't mean I'm unwilling to help. This is heavy! This is dangerous! Let me grab this end. Wait, I'm twisted; I need to change my hands. I was going to clear a space for this. Wait! Ugh, Dad, why didn't you wait for me? If you ask me to help, you have to be willing to let it happen outside of your time line!"

On and on. I just went off. I was so annoyed at him and the stubborn self-centered time line his actions demanded that I conform to. Then I stopped. After I cooled off (and the sewing machine was safely down the stairs), I asked myself the questions I hate to ask myself the most: "Why am I so pissed? What was *that* about? What is it about Dad's behavior that is *just like me?*"

I was so over-the-top irritated by him in that moment I had to consider I may actually be seeing an aspect of myself I was unwilling to face. I let that sit inside my head for about thirty seconds, and then the mirror appeared. Ding, ding, ding! We have a winner. I do the same exact shit to my daughter, to my ex-husband, to anyone I try to delegate work to who doesn't do it fast enough. I was ashamed and needed to apologize for my outburst.

The mirror showed me that I'm a fairly unforgiving taskmaster when I ask someone to do something—like unload the dishwasher, clean their room, or put away the clothes. If they don't do it fast enough, I just do it for them, sometimes with a dramatic flair. And then, of course, let's not forget my corresponding resentment. "Oh, never mind. I'll just do it," has come out of my mouth at least once or twice a zillion times.

Once I see this in the mirror, I need to accept that I'm in the position to consciously make a change. No small task.

Wanting things done on my timetable is a mainstay of my existence, but now that I can see it, and more important, see a layer of how the person on the other end might feel, it is my responsibility to work on that. It sucks.

So will you choose to work on the tough stuff? Totally up to you! Nevertheless, I can provide a structure here for you to find the things you can begin with and help you start small. I suggest you write about each day. Sit for a moment, after dinner perhaps, and reflect on the events of your day. Pay attention to the difficult days, the sucky, bristly ones. They have a message for you as long as you can examine them without reliving them! Write about those moments as if you were a bystander. Write about the funny ways the day's word popped into your mind. What were you doing, thinking, or avoiding? Write about the people you saw, the things they said, and whether or not it circled you back to your word.

If you don't journal, there is a list at the end of the book. When you finish a day, take some time to reflect and put a few notes on the list.

Was the day an easy one? Was it so easy it made your heart sing? Take notes, and put a big star on this day. Then set the list aside.

Did the day keep presenting you with a multitude of problems to get in the way, so much so that you considered skipping that day altogether? Pay attention to that day.

Keep notes of what the struggles were that day, and then set the list aside.

Was the day neither fun nor difficult? Did you catch yourself saying, "Nothing new here," or, "Meh, what's the big deal?" Take a few notes, and set the list aside.

When all twenty-six days are finished, take a day or two away from your list. Then come back and get to work. For now, though, let's get started at the beginning, A all the way to Z. Twenty-six adventures are waiting!

A is for Accept

The first thing to embrace here is that acceptance does *not* imply approval of, agreement with, admiration of, or any type of absolution. It only means, "It is." For today, as each thing unfolds, accept it without judgment—good or bad, ugly or pretty, thick or thin, hot or cold, or disaster or miracle. It just is, and it is simply unfolding for you.

Being able to accept things into my world—as they are—is not a skill developed overnight. This is not for wimps. This is perhaps one of the hardest things I do on an ongoing basis. In small doses, though, I can stop myself from overreacting to things and remind myself to just let them be. When I can do this, my life ultimately calms down. Worrying about anything has never—*not once*—changed the outcome of what I obsessively worried about: paying bills, divorce, motherhood, my job, my weight, my aging reflection, my pets, my car, my dad, my daughter, and so on. This list is really infinite, right?

Every event, disaster, or life trauma has a moment when you can choose to accept that the event has entered or occurred in your life. It is vital you feel the difference between acceptance and approval; they are not the same. And if this event is a trauma in your life caused by another person, it is also important to know that acceptance does not mean you approve of or condone this asshole's choice to harm you.

Bad things have happened. Some were due to my errors, and others were and will be due to mistakes of others. I often take on the responsibilities of the world and somehow think that my intervention, my action, my inaction, or my worry can somehow alter reality and make it all better.

Wow. What a fantasy world I live in. *Who do I think I am?*

I think this is the curse of a caregiver/survivor, but my need to somehow magically prevent bad things from happening can interfere with my ability to let life unfold, or my ability to accept the reality that bad things have already happened.

This is not healthy.

Acceptance feels like a release of tension, tension from pushing and pulling to try to erase what happened, to change the past, or to control the future, a person, or a situation. All, of course, are impossible tasks. Believing and acting as if you have any of that power or control constricts like rope twisting head to toes. It's exhausting.

Acceptance is the moment you feel the rope release and drop to the floor.

Whatever happens this one day, don't give it a label. The dog shits on the carpet? It's simply a pile of poo on the floor that needs cleaning. Clean, and move on. It happened. You can't unpoop it. Accepting that it happened doesn't imply you approve of your dog doing this, or that you're delighted by the experience. It simply happened. Breathe through it.

The car won't start? Breathe through it. Make a list of who you need to call. The appointment you will miss? Someone to come give your battery a jump? A taxi service? Breathe. Accept that at this instant, the car doesn't start. Don't judge. Don't overreact and decide this is the worst event ever. You can't possibly know that's true. A giant semi full of battery acid could be heading for a tragic accident involving your car at this very moment had the car started. Or maybe not. You don't know; maybe your stupid, not working car just saved your life.

Flat tire?

Overslept?

Child home sick from school?

Toilet overflow?

Nothing lasts forever. No one event will consume the rest of your living days, unless, of course, you let it because you have chosen to let it live on in your thoughts and inner monologue as if it had a tiny apartment in your head.

For this twenty-four-hour period, if it comes, accept it. Try saying this: "Today I will accept this event as it is. If it needs a plan to resolve it, I will make that plan, or I will find someone to help me make the plan. If I can't do anything about it, then we're done here. This is my day, not *its* day!"

B is for Breathe

Take a deep breath. Fill your belly. If you can't feel your stomach expand, then you have to lie back down in bed. On your back, you can't help but fill your diaphragm. Breathe in.

Hold the breath. Hold it for three or four Mississippis. Let it out slowly.

Repeat. Breathe in, and fill that belly. Hold the breath. Let it out slowly.

Now you're allowed to get out of bed or move from the couch, office chair, or room.

My chest and belly get so tight sometimes that I realize I'm actually holding my breath! Let the air flow through you today. Hold on to none of it in a nervous, anxious way.

When you breathe like this, you give yourself a moment of power in a world where so many things leave you feeling powerless. Controlling your breath in a world, day, or moment when you feel *nothing* is under control can grant you a peaceful moment. Permit yourself that peaceful, powerful moment.

I hold my tension in my gut. The tightness there holds hands with my need to control things. I'm not 100 percent sure it's about control, but it feels like it's my wish to change things that can't be changed or to avoid things I don't want to deal with. Whatever it is, that tension follows me through my day as I move from task to task and from responsibility to responsibility. All the while, the voice in my head narrates my life, asking, *Why this? Why that? Why not this? Why not that?*

I catch myself holding my breath sometimes, and it feels almost as if I forgot to breathe. Not healthy. Breathing is one of those things that the body just does thousands of times a day, whether you're paying attention or not, and filling your lungs isn't the same as filling your belly. You have a moment to take control of twenty seconds of your life by simply stopping and thinking about the air you breathe in and the air you breathe out. For me, twenty seconds in charge may be the only twenty seconds I get today to not feel helpless, powerless, or underutilized.

The benefits of giving yourself those twenty seconds is cumulative. The more often you can take a moment in the day to breathe, the more you begin to untie knots of tension and release a few worries here and there. It may actually blend quite well with your ability to accept things.

As you move throughout your day, natural transitions will occur, such as rising from your table or desk, heading to a meeting, heading to the bathroom, preparing your child for a nap, preparing to go to the library, getting out of your car, turning off the television before heading to bed, and on and on and on. Before you transition from one event to the next, take a moment and breathe in and out two times. I don't ask that you clear your mind and try to not think. Go ahead and think about what you're transitioning to, but see if you can fill your belly two times before heading into that next thing.

If you miss a transition moment, so what? Worrying about missing the transition or whether you're doing it right ruins the entire gift of controlling your own twenty seconds. If you get in four deep-breathing transitions today, that is probably four more than yesterday, so rock on!

Try saying this at your next transition: "I will take these breaths. They are mine to enjoy."

C is for Compassion

A day of compassion can be exhausting, so gear up.

What is compassion? *Dictionary.com* defines compassion as "a feeling of deep sympathy and sorrow for another who is stricken by misfortune, accompanied by a strong desire to alleviate the suffering." When I asked my phone, the nice lady inside defined it as "sympathetic pity and concern for the sufferings or misfortunes of others."

The word "pity" causes me discomfort. I don't believe anyone needs my pity. We all have bad days. We have all been victims, we have all been hurt, we have all been upset, and personally, pity never made me feel any better. Not once.

My view on the definition is really about understanding that we each have these struggles of suffering or misfortune. I don't need to understand your struggle or even agree with how you are handling your struggle. I just need to understand that you *have* the struggle. That is my compassion toward you.

What might that feel like for a day? It's the way I feel when I'm sending someone a tiny wish of loving-kindness, hope, or just sunshine. But before we go too far, I think we should send ourselves some compassion in order to get started. I imagine over the course of just the first two days you fell short once or twice. Perhaps you failed to accept something that really pissed you off and you're still stewing it over, or the breathing exercise just got in the way, which is funny because it also kept you alive. But no matter. Send yourself a compassionate inner smile, and let the need to stew over your didn't-do-it list fade away. The reason I ask you to consider this is because the person I tend to forget to be compassionate toward the most is me. I'm guessing you forget yourself too.

I realize that a traditional definition of compassion implies that the other party is suffering or in discomfort of some kind. But I want to view the world through the focus of what I am offering or sending to another, regardless of his or her situation. Certainly, it does seem that the suffering or sadness gets my tiny wishes more often, but I like to focus on what's in my heart as I make eye contact with someone and have peace cross my mind and face.

So for today, we're going to focus on sending those tiny wishes out into the world. We will send thoughts of love, peace, tranquility, kindness, and sunshine out to anyone and everyone we cross paths with—even if we don't understand this person or agree with the way he or she behaves.

Full disclosure, there are also real moments I struggle being compassionate toward others. When anger creeps in, I need to send those wishes even more. But I have to pause and take a moment to remind myself to do so. When some assbasket cuts me off in traffic and scares my daughter or me, my need to swear battles my need to send compassion. When compassion wins, my internal or external response is usually, "I hope they arrive safely and that everyone they're heading to see is safe." I don't know what the other driver's life is like. I don't know why he or she is in such a damn hurry. My anger won't change any of the other person's circumstances, but what if my calm thoughts of loving-kindness float alongside that person's car? What if?

For today, look around you, find the folks who need your silent wish of compassionate kindness, and send it off on the breeze. The homeless guy on the corner, the coworker who irritates you, the boss who shouts at you, the child standing alone on the playground, the tired-looking man or woman with the world heavy on their shoulders. There are multitudes of people who for no reason at all just need a simple wish of happiness, joy, peace, and love. Be the sender today. Grant them that wish.

Send it with a small smile, and go about your day. You never know what you may have just set in motion.

D is for Divinity

Divinity: I don't believe this word will mean the same thing for any two people, so define it as you will. But for one day, I would like you to concentrate on the miracle that is *you*.

The fact that you exist at all is simply an amazing thing. All the events, people, and places that had to intersect in order to combine the perfect molecular stew that is you is a pretty phenomenal event if you ask me.

You see the world in only one way—your way. No one else matches that. We will cross paths with people we agree with, disagree with, understand, and don't understand, but there is no one else who looks through your eyes and perceives the world the way you do.

Because of this unique miracle, I choose to view each of us as a tiny spark of the divine. We are all part of this much larger mass of tiny sparks composed of our individual special pieces of the Divinity. Some of us are gifted speakers, artists, healers, writers, conversationalists, protectors, nurturers, thinkers, problems solvers, caregivers, listeners, dancers, smilers, organizers, and huggers. And some are excellent laughers. Have you ever been around a person whose laughter fills you up? I have, and I'm warmed from the inside out after we cross paths.

Since this list of our individual gifts is infinite, and since we can't each be *all* of these things in one healthy body without being probably insane and not knowing which way to go with our lives, I believe we each bring our own sprinkling of gifts from the infinite list. It is by being in the presence of others with different sprinklings that we gain balance and joy. When I'm in need of support, I seek my friends with the gifts of encouragement, insight, and empathy. When others need clarity, they seek my logic, organization, and creativity. We balance each other out and fill in the gaps.

What are your special sprinkles? Before you begin your day, try to think of at least five. If you have trouble coming up with five, dig deeper—or call me. I bet I can listen to you for ten minutes and know what makes you awesome! Maybe it's your smile, your glowing eyes, your patience, your ability to doodle and talk on the phone simultaneously, or the crow's feet that demonstrate a lifetime of smiling. Or maybe it's your quiet demeanor that calms those around you, or your ability to be the life of the party and tell a great joke. You have sprinkles, I'm sure, simply because of the fact that you exist—period.

Take a risk today, and ask a few people what it is about you that they admire. Here are a few sentence starters: "Why do you think we're friends? Is there anything about me you see as an admirable trait?" You may be surprised by what the people who surround you on a daily basis might say when asked a sincere question. It can help you take a moment to look at your reflection through someone else's eyes. Don't let modesty or denial respond with, "No, I'm not." Whatever it is they see in you is their perspective, and a simple, "Really? Thank you," is all that's required. Keep a running list. This list can become a bookmark to pull out whenever you feel insecure, unsteady, unready, or just plain "not enough." You have left an impression on the people around you, and those are the bits of divinity that they get to take with them after crossing paths with you.

Today, spread your divine pieces around. When encountering others who have the tiny pieces I need, and I have the tiny pieces they need, it is not an exchange I can see, but it's an exchange I can feel. Consider, "When I come in contact with you, what missing pieces of divinity are we sharing with each other today?"

E is for Epiphany

For today, try to remember an instance when your brain just clicked, and you said, "Ohhh, I get it," or perhaps a, "Yes! I got it!"

That spontaneous moment when the perfect idea or solution to a problem just popped in your head, bringing with it a moment of great release and joy. The mystery has been solved. The veil lifted for a moment, and all was good. I imagine at other times there can be a release of tears and sorrow; that has happened to me as well after an epiphany. Regardless, the moment is sudden, and it tends to create a release—release of confusion, stress, struggle, pain, conflict, or any blockage that has been holding you back.

My moments of epiphany typically occur around a problem I have or a puzzle that needs solving at work. Nearly every time the epiphany finally arrives within the twenty-four-hour period that I "gave up" on it, and my mind is like, *Nope, we're not doing this anymore.* I don't mean that I've given up forever, but I have temporarily admitted defeat and decided to set it aside for a bit and think about something else. As I sift through other problems, or sit staring at something, it is the grace of Spirit that whispers inside my head and all of a sudden, I just know this will work!

Funny thing about that Spirit that inspires, it knows when I'm faking. It seems to know when I pretend to give up on the problem just to see if it will bring me the answer. The key is to truly, with all your heart and soul, walk away from the problem and dig into something else.

What I love about these moments is the coinciding amnesia that comes with it. You forever get it, and the way it felt to be so confused and seeking are just gone. It reminds me of those illusions you stare at until you see the faces or the horse or whatever it is you're supposed to find. Once you find them, you can never go back. You can never unfind them. For the rest of your life, when you see that tree picture, you will always see the faces hidden within.

My wish for you today is that perhaps you actually have an epiphany during the day. Unfortunately, part of the accepted definition of "epiphany" has the words, "a rare occurrence," in it, so perhaps today won't be the day. But what if it is? Oh, how wonderful.

As you begin your day, say, "Today I will release my need to know the answers or the direction to take. Today I am letting the right answers just appear in my quiet, unassuming mind."

F is for Faith

Faith can be difficult. I should say faith is difficult for me sometimes. To trust, rely, and believe with unwavering conviction often challenges me. The faith I'm talking about is complete trust and confidence in someone. Not specifically religious faith.

So for today, the focus is on faith in someone, specifically, faith in you. Faith in how strong and capable you are. Today, believe in yourself before you decide to put your faith in someone else. Those empty spaces we have that don't contain the faith in ourselves that we *can* handle it, *can* do it, *can* accomplish it are the exact spaces that, at times, get taken over and manipulated by others to be used as *they* please. These people may be wonderfully kind and offer to help you in your hour of need, and they are likely full of good intentions. But why not first believe in your own ability to help yourself and then call on others to assist you. Remember, it's just for one day.

For some, like me, it is difficult to ask for help because it is difficult to trust. Other times, it is difficult to ask for help because you have no idea what to ask for. Having faith in yourself first leads you to ask the right questions. The right questions to ask, and the specific help to ask for, come much easier once you have already started to work on the situation yourself because now you know what your needs are and can put a name to what is hindering your progress.

The moment you tell yourself, "I just can't do this," and let others in without first looking through your eyes of experience can send you in directions that you blindly follow. Then halfway in, your gut says no, and everyone tilts their heads at you and replies, "But you said you needed help!"

Having faith for a single day can get you through a surprisingly long list of difficult circumstances. It has served me well in certain situations, mostly out of necessity and isolation, and secondly out of a stubborn quality I have of wanting to handle things on my own first. But what I have learned from experience is that having the faith that you can handle what comes—be it a job loss, a death in the family, a broken bone, a car accident, a broken heart, an addiction, an assault, whatever life throws at you—is possible and important. There is no reason that my little list can't apply to you too.

Have faith that you will be able to handle what comes your way. Don't give your crisis away to someone else to handle for you too quickly. Asking for help and support is important, but if you give your struggle away too quickly, you have just given away life's greatest opportunity to learn exactly how strong you really are. You can earn a new badge of supreme courage. Imagine yourself in a decorated coat of armor. You truly can handle it. You may have lots of tears and pain, and time may seem to move in slow motion, but you can handle it. Have faith that you are never alone, never isolated, never not capable—you are able to own your crisis or problem, and once you believe that you're able to learn from it, you know exactly how to seek the appropriate help without giving away your opportunity to learn. After all, if you turn inward to trust in yourself and link that to a spiritual faith, where do you suppose all that inner strength comes from?

Having faith in myself is a big opportunity for growth, and I want it for you too. If for just one day I focus on trusting the day to take me where I need to go, having enough faith in myself to make it through the day with good choices, then I can smile through the day. My goal will be to link a bunch of these single days together and create a confident, trusting life filled with trustworthy friends, loyal confidants, and faith in the beauty and madness of it all.

Today say, "I have faith in me today, and if it rains, so be it; this I can handle."

G is for Generosity

Generosity of spirit is where to place our focus today.

For much of 2013 and 2014, I was running on empty in the financial arena. I needed to live on $1,700 a month. I took care of the rent, utilities, and groceries. For my daughter and me, there was no room for big, fun, crazy bonus buys in my near future. It wasn't too painful for me because I'm not much of a big spender anyway; I was still wearing a Carhart coat over fifteen years old for my winter gear.

The moments when I wished I could spend more typically stemmed from parental guilt, wishing that I could offer more to my daughter, who didn't really seem to notice one way or the other at the time.

This is where generosity comes in. This word has always sent my mind straight to money, but I needed to do some inner work to realize it applies to so much more. When money was at its tightest, I had to focus on ways I could be generous that had nothing to do with money. Back then, if I had loose change in the car or a few singles handy, then yes, I handed them out the car window to the firefighters

19

holding the boots. On other days, I couldn't because those extra singles were necessary for the next week's field trip fee. It was a balance of financial and emotional generosity. For me, I had to learn to be okay with not being able to be financially generous all the time, and not being financially generous has always had a ton of built-in guilt and shame that I'm still working on.

I learned to be generous with my smile when I was out and about. Here is how that works. In the store, if I see someone who looks completely sad and defeated, I make eye contact. I give a smile with a hint of "Been there, done that, got the T-shirt." If I can pull a hint of relief from the person's face, then my generosity has been received.

I learned to be generous with my time. Spending extra moments really listening can be one of the most generous things I do in a day. It is about quietly being present for someone. I still spend extra moments with anyone needing to share a story with me. Sometimes it's the crazy old dude in the coffee shop, telling me how to live my life, or sometimes it's my neighbor with the "guy troubles." My favorite extra time is with my daughter, listening to her tell me a story while we run errands or just sitting near her when she does homework.

I also, maybe reluctantly, learned to be generous with my prayers. My method is to send off a positive loving thought when I'm feeling uneasy, annoyed, or scared. A fire truck blasts by loud and scary, and I say, "I hope everyone's okay."

Someone drives around me dangerously cutting through traffic, and I say, "I hope you arrive safely." Whoever I come across during the day who needs some extra love, I simply send off a little prayer. My prayers aren't a typical prayer like I learned when I was a child because, as you will soon know, the word "prayer" gives me a considerable amount of discomfort. In my world, I just take a moment to send a focused thought of pure goodness, hope, and love.

Your generosity goal for the day is to give of yourself, your heart, your smile, your time, your ears instead of your dollars. This form of generosity pays itself back instantaneously. You might get to hear a fascinating story, make a new friend, or quite possibly extend some emotional relief to someone who was in desperate need.

Two more fun things for you to do are (a) come up with as many nonfinancial generosities as you can, and (b) come up with your "to be funded" list. Make a list of the various charities you want to recognize. Create the list, and do what you can when you can. Sometimes your generosity of time for an organization is where the real need is, and then other times, it is the generosity of cash. My inner growth around my relationship with money has required that I lose my mind-set of, "If I can't give money, I can't give anything. Therefore, I'm a bad person."

I continue to dig deep and work through my poverty mind-set and fear of the almighty dollar (or lack thereof). But the process of creating my lists creates the opportunity of visualizing the process of giving both financially and personally. As I talk with my daughter about which organizations she is interested in, we can both see the needs and the opportunities that each of us can support. Staying in this mind-set of generosity gives us the chance to remember it doesn't have to be an all or nothing idea.

Today say, "I will give whatever I can to whoever I can whenever I can."

H Is for Heart

Today we focus on the center of our chests. That fist-sized beating heart that feels as if it has a purpose so much grander than as a pumping system.

Pay close attention to all the feelings in your chest today. Whenever you can, place your attention there; choose an image that makes you smile. Imagine a rose blossom—any color—opening as in time-lapse photography. Imagine blue-green fairy dust falling onto a beautiful leaf; this is where you can tell I over watched Tinker Bell movies when my daughter was younger. Alternatively, you can imagine two hands gently cupping your heart as it glows a beautiful color of your choosing. Whatever color lights up in your imagination is just fine. I'm sure you can think of an image that will redirect your focus to the center of your chest, away from all the mind chatter that distracts you.

The heart is an amazing organ. I have felt the pain of my heart breaking from sadness, despair, and disappointment. But I have also felt my heart swell from the joy of pride, love, or amazement.

Does my physical heart literally swell or break? I have no idea, but to feel those sensations is certainly experience enough to warrant my respect, tenderness, and attention for the day.

It is also there in my heart space that warns me of my tendency to live in a place of fear. My heart has become my reality checker. I will feel a nervous fluttering that might be considered panic. That flutter used to scare the shit out of me, but now I use it as a reminder that there is a distinct possibility that my imagination has run away with me and taken me on a worst-case adventure. I'm an expert worst-case scenario thinker. It's how I solve problems. I see the worst case, and then I work backward to create a plan to avoid it. This ignores my heart and heads straight to my brain.

A system of troubleshooting backward design works great for the workplace but not so much for the personal life. During the day, if you feel the flutter, try to pause, breathe, and reconsider the nervous thoughts flying through your head. Panic usually comes from worrying about the worst. In my experience, not one single worst imagining I have run through my head has actually happened as bad as I played it out in my head. I'm exceptionally creative at taking any worry down a path that ends in some layer of death or destruction. Return to your heart.

Worrying about what-if has wasted more of my time than I care to admit. Thinking about all the what-ifs that filled my mind, and then comparing those to what actually transpired, almost in a T-chart format, has helped me see that nothing turned out the way I thought it might. Not one thing. Return to your heart.

Things I have been panic-stricken about have, for the most part, turned out not as scary as I assumed they would. I'm not saying that they weren't scary. Some were, but they were different scary than the drama my mind was able to create. Here is a sampling of my scary: being a single mother, breaking a bone, losing my house, failing at anything, succeeding at anything, leaving a job, bankruptcy, getting a job, dating, dying alone. All these things I have spent hours worrying about. Imaging the worst. Spinning the stories of defeat, pain, humiliation, anger, drama, and disappointment was so much heavier *and* worse than the *actual* run-of-the-mill pain, humiliation, anger, drama, and disappointment that I ended up feeling once I pulled my head out of my fear and let life happen. Aside from dying alone, which I can now only assume won't be nearly as bad as I imagine it, my head hijacked every one of those situations and made them worse. My heart was never engaged, and it should have been.

Pulling my head out of my fear is actually paying attention to my heart aching. I would feel the ache—I still do at times—and the feeling reminds me to breathe through my heart and be still. It is beating, and I am capable. I have to remind myself of this often, and my heart is where I find that reminder. To focus on the heart can pull the story your mind tells you back into a place of pure love and balance. It is a quality messenger of feeling, not imagination.

Focus on your heart; return to the image you chose. Breathe and appreciate your heart's power as an unbiased messenger of sorrow, warning, reality check, and love.

I is for Imagination

I love it when it is so quiet I can hear the snow falling.

I love it when I see a shooting star.

What tiny moments do you love? Not because you receive their gifts every day but precisely because you don't.

These tiny, seldom-occurring events are the kinds of moments you can use to exercise your imagination, the act of remembering, imagining, reliving the rare and precious. It's exercise for your brain, mind, and heart. I have to close my eyes to hear the snow in my memory, but I can keep them open to see the memory of a shooting star. I think that's weird. If I close my eyes, my ears tingle as I think, *Snowfall*, and if I open my eyes, the image of a shooting star floats in my imagination somewhere above this page I'm looking at. It almost seems to be floating in a bubble above my head. I love the way imagination works.

The imagination can certainly be used to create brand-new, never before seen things, sounds, objects, solutions, and so on. But I like to think that I am more likely to imagine that great new thing if I use my imagination often—giving it practice so to speak. So I exercise mine by filling my imagination with details from things I remember, but I don't worry about accuracy. It might seem like I'm exercising my memory, but it's more than that. I don't just remember something; it's the practice of filling my mind with sounds and pictures that I can really see that helps me improve my imagination. I have practiced hearing snow falling so much that I am now able to close my eyes and hear it when I'm in a crowded place, feeling overwhelmed or about to panic. It helps me feel centered and calm.

I wonder, I imagine, I create. Something as simple as the alphabet started me wondering, wondering if I could find words to live by in a simple list. Admittedly, the fact that I want a list to live by hints to you I'm sure that I am a bit of a control freak, or that I want things in life to be a tidy, manageable to-do list. And I guess I am ... and I do. That doesn't mean I am without imagination, though. Nor are you. Sitting with your mind and taking charge of the story and images you fill it with can be a wonderful break from the daily stresses that overwhelm.

I won't lie; my mind does take advantage of "running me" every now and then, and it is terrifying. My mind can imagine horrible scenarios and outcomes that paralyze me or send me off into imagined panic or shame. If I catch myself quickly and stop, breathe, imagine the snow, the birth of my daughter, or light reflecting on water, I take back control over my mind. And in that moment, I have victory over the willy-nilly chattering of my mind. The challenge is to take over more quickly than the panic grows. I'm not the best yet, but I'm working on it.

Think about a beautiful moment you remember seeing or hearing. What colors do you see? What sounds? What smells can you remember? Close your eyes if it helps.

That moment you are imagining belongs only to you. It's like a rare privilege that you were graciously once invited to witness, and now it is being imagined all over again by you. It adds a whole new level of special to your moment.

All things are perceived in only one way—your way. The tricky part here is that it happens for *each* of us, which is probably why there are so many misunderstandings. Your memory, your moment is unique to you. Mine is unique to me. Fascinating. I think that makes these moments true treasures to behold and definitely worth spending at least sixty seconds with each day to exercise your imagination. How about you?

Try it every chance you get today. Invite your imagination in for the day, and enjoy your ability to create sights, sounds, smells, color, and music inside your private inner space. Don't try it while driving; a boring meeting is okay though. Operating heavy machinery—no. Listening to someone drone on and on about the effective growth of cost analysis—yes. What does that even mean?

J is for Joy

Be joyful today! This is your tenth day of your twenty-six days to practice peace. If you have placed your focus on any of the previous nine words, I am hopeful that you found joy. Or at the very least, a small bit of comfort at some point during one or more of your days.

Being joyful is something that feels "bouncier" to me than being happy feels. I don't know why that is. A smiling baby seems to embody joy. Grover, my eighty-pound Newfoundland mix seemed joyful when he used to hop around in the snow.

Joy also seems to have a distinct look and feel to it and is easy to spot. But it's not a simple task I'm asking of you. Memories of joy are much easier to tap into than creating a moment of joy on the spot. If creating joy on the spot were that easy, I'm pretty sure my life would be so different I wouldn't recognize it. Let's start easily with memories.

Before I headed back to the working world a few years ago, I would stand at the kitchen door and watch my daughter walk across the yard, out the gate, across the street toward her friend's house, looking back to wave multiple times on her way to school. I felt joy watching her. It was different than just being happy; it was an internal understanding that these moments would soon be gone and that I had better soak up the feelings of these mornings and make them last. I had stood at that door every morning since she let me know it was no longer acceptable to have her mom walk her to school. Also, since I knew my morning time to watch her was coming to an end, I was able to cultivate the joyful feeling as I watched her head off to school.

Tears of joy are also things to cherish. A moment so wonderful that your eyes leak; there's nothing quite like that. Tears of sorrow or shame sting my eyes. They make it too cloudy to see as I typically drop my gaze to hide my face and walk away. Not tears of joy, though. They are light, crystal-clear, and almost refreshing to my eyes.

I am trying to think of a recent moment when I had tears of joy; I am exercising my imagination. But I am struggling right now because I have had more of those painful, stinging tears lately. There has been more sorrow lately than joy, but I rely on the fact that nothing is forever. Here is another peek into why I needed to start writing my *26 Days to Practice Peace*. Making lists, writing, thinking, wondering are all things I do to jump-start myself out of a sorrow spiral.

Today the focus will be joy. The joy I feel when I see my child after work. The joy I feel when I know I made a difference in someone's day. The joy I feel when I make someone laugh at work with my goofy comments, and the joy I feel when I watch my daughter from across the room while she's busy being a child. Fleeting moments. Joyful fleeting moments. In the midst of a sorrow spiral, when my heart feels heavy or defeated, I must stop and remember joy.

Stop for a moment, and find a memory with "bounce." For many, those memories exist fairly far back in our lives. For others, it was yesterday when you nearly peed while laughing. Find your own bouncy memory of joy, and return to it often today.

I wish each of you all the joy in the world today.

K is for Kindness

There is one consistent rule in our home: Be kind. Now, I break this rule way more than I care to admit, but I am quick to apologize, point out my lack of sensitivity, and try to make it better as soon as I can. To be kind for one day is achievable, but it's always the day I choose to focus on kindness that all the irritating crap (that is, people) confronts me in order to test my resolve. Every person and every problem pokes at me as if to ask, "Do you really mean it? Are you going to be kind? Even if I do this? Or this? What about this?"

My desire to focus on kindness stems from a very awkward adolescence that consisted of many insecure moments, a great deal of teasing, a lot of not fitting in, and being told by others that I didn't fit in for their amusement. As well as some all-around mean people doing their best to make me feel small and insignificant by maybe, say, yanking my gym shorts down as the boys PE class ran by. Today we call that bullying. Back then I called it my life.

These experiences turned me into the All-Around-Root-for-the-Underdog Queen of Empathy. I'm considering getting myself a tiara and sash. As a child, I watched *It's the Great Pumpkin, Charlie Brown* every single year, hoping that Charlie Brown would not get a rock and wanting desperately to squeeze myself into the TV just to be his friend, share my candy, and never pull the football away from him if I ever got a chance to meet him.

The reason my teaching career primarily resided within the middle-school years was my wanting to be a "protector" for anyone feeling awkward, intimidated, insecure, or vulnerable—which pretty much describes the entire early-adolescent experience. To make sure no one was ever treated as I had been. It would be great to say I was always successful, but I know I wasn't. The classrooms, hallways, and lunchtimes of the world are terrifying places for students who resemble a younger version of me.

I encourage empathy from my daughter as well, but I got lucky. She was wired this way from the start, so I can't really claim that I taught her anything about being kind. When she was younger, I would point out situations on TV or in real life where we could talk about how alone or sad or embarrassed someone might feel, and what I would do to make the person feel better. She would add her own ideas as well. I also encouraged her to notice kids at school who look lost or lonely and to say a quick "Hi" if she felt comfortable doing that.

Being kind to someone else never implies that we have to be "besties." It implies that I value you enough to extend my best behavior. By doing so, there's a small chance the person might return the favor to you or someone else. I'm just hoping that if I remember to be kind, hold my acid tongue, and not feed into anyone else's lack of kindness, that my overall area of existence will start to become a better place for me, my daughter, and anyone willing to visit my corner of the world.

I'm hoping that my kind corner of the world will touch each of your kind corners, and we can each breathe giant sighs of relief. Keep an eye on each other today, and be the kind protector of those you see. Are there people in your world who need a kindness? Smile, say hello, and let them know you see them. Remember, though, that if you take this challenge, all the irritating crap that is testing your resolve may confront you too. So if you feel the irritation rise, breathe deep and say to yourself, "Today I will be kind."

L is for Love

I entered an essay contest once about love. Specifically, I had to write about a time I learned the meaning of love. The more I thought, the more baffled I became by this task.

The meaning of love? What love? Romantic love, unconditional love, passionate love, brotherly love, platonic love, true love, lasting love? What about the love I have for my pets, nature, or my old truck? The more I thought about it, the bigger and more confusing the word "love" became to me. I tend to overthink things.

Each love on my list had a very different experience attached to it. Some of them I had multiple and varying experiences with—some painful, some not. I just couldn't quite articulate a single moment I learned the meaning of love, so I wrote about helping my then eight-year-old daughter learn to look at the difficult bits of our world, like poverty, mental illness, and homelessness, with her own eyes in a gentle and loving way. I was proud of my losing essay.

Honest feelings of love are, of course, wonderful sensations. They are wonderful places to live. Any aspect of love, any version of love, and any moment of sharing love is important. I no longer stress about romantic love. I was young once and enjoyed that experience, but that ship has sailed. Now I focus on motherly love, the love I extend to friends in need, and my ability to demonstrate love by accepting others and circumstances without judgment.

It seems to me that learning the meaning of love is a lifelong activity. I didn't understand the feelings of unconditional love until I was thirty-eight, when my daughter was born. And I am still learning about selfless love as I watch others giving so much of themselves, expecting nothing in return. To have learned how selfless love feels, I know I'm not consistently there yet.

Have you noticed what's missing from my list? It may be because I'm the worst at it and because it hasn't become part of my inner vocabulary yet. Love of oneself. Even as I ponder the list of loves, this one got passed over and became an afterthought as I write. That right there is the problem! Putting oneself on the list of loves as an afterthought! That habit of treating ourselves as afterthoughts is probably the root cause of many struggles and conflicts.

We need to cultivate a love for ourselves that won't accept poor treatment from others or poor treatment from ourselves. No inner putdowns, name-calling, or inner judgments. For twenty-four hours, every time you catch yourself thinking or saying something negative about yourself, just say, "Oops, sorry," and stop. Don't dwell on it; apologize to yourself and move on. This is one very difficult habit to break. I know because I am still struggling very much here. I can honestly say that right now, as of today, I still do not know how this love feels. Of course, I imagine it to be this awesome wave of love, similar to unconditional, that will just wash over me one day when I least expect it. I am guessing it will be life-changing and will open me up to other kinds of love in the process. But I'm just not there yet, and that is also okay.

I'm certain love is big enough to keep teaching us for the rest of time.

M is for Meditate

Ugh. How I wish I could do it "right." I know it really is silly to put rules on something as wonderful as taking a moment to feel still. The rules totally defeat the whole purpose of feeling still. So stop putting rules on it. But I want to be "right" and "perfect." Does that sound familiar?

I don't want to offend any masters of meditation, but if you're anything like me—a beginner *and* a perfectionist— the mere fact that you're "not doing it right" makes you stop all together and walk away (for years possibly) because you would rather not try at all than fail. There, I said it. That's me in a nutshell.

I have decided that my mind-set is stifling and stupid. In celebration of my decision, I have once again picked up my practice of sitting still and listening to my breathing. When I first started two years ago, my goal was ten- to twenty-minute "sits" four days a week. Over the past two years, my success moved forward and backward, good days, bad days, no days.

My optimal time was to do it in the morning, during the time before I needed to make sure my daughter was up for school but after I showered and had some coffee. I sat on my bed, leaned against my pillow against the wall, eyes usually closed, trying to sit straight, crossed legs— sometimes, hands in my lap or on my knees. I would take a big breath in and let out a huge sigh. This would get me started because my ability to hear that giant sigh reminded me to stop listening to my crazy mind talk. I would listen to my breathing as long as I could still hear it before my mind started talking again, which might have only been five seconds or, on a good day, twenty. Then, when I realized I was "talking" again, I switched over to thinking, "In … Out … In … Out," alongside my breathing, until that got boring. Then I tried hearing my breathing again. That would work for a bit and then I would return to thinking in and out all over.

This process would go on until I screamed inside, and my eyes popped open. I usually laughed and tried to not beat myself up about it. Some is always more than none.

Currently, I have found a nice app on my phone to help me focus for ten to even thirty minutes, and I have successfully had a quiet meditation session for 325 days in a row. My problem is that now I'm not entirely convinced about my reasons to continue because the app tracks days in a row and gives me little imaginary awards. And because I have issues, I wonder am now motivated to meditate only out of spite because I don't want to lose my days in a row streak?

Ridiculous, I know, but honest. Again, some is always more than none when it comes to sit time. So I continue and hope that I grow out of my compulsion to not break my streak. Maybe when I hit 365 days in a row I will retire it.

Sometimes I try at night when I'm lying down, getting ready for bed. It even puts me to sleep occasionally, so I don't know if I can really count that as meditation. But I'm not following rules anymore, right?

Good luck, everyone. It's really just breathing, and your body already does that. So try to find a quiet moment today to sit. I hope your moment can pull all your stray pieces back to center and give you a sturdy start to your day!

N is for Now

I am not completely gifted at "being in the now" yet, but I work at it enough to know that being in the now pulls me out of panic attacks, worry, unrealistic expectations, and most of all, my tendency to try to predict my future.

My ability to predict my future, however, actually super-sucks. I could fill countless pages with all the things I thought "today" would be like, going all the way back to my childhood, when I assumed that being fifty was blue hair, support hose, and wrinkles. Or my predictions that I would live out West and ride cross country on the back of a motorcycle driven by my husband, who happened to look just like the 1974 Marlboro Man.

What I didn't predict was where I really am, happily living in Ohio with my daughter and my father, teaching college students who want to be teachers, writing my heart out, and occasionally experimenting with my love of paper and paper filigree. Where I am *not* is with the Marlboro Man, not a model, not a Radio City Rockette, not an actress of stage or screen, not a middle-school principal, not an accountant, and not living in Wyoming or Alaska like I had previously predicted at one time or another over the past fifty years.

I had all sorts of fun predictions, but for every fun prediction, I have also predicted horrible things for my future as well. These predictions typically fall into various stories of poverty, isolation, and illness. They are the scary scenarios I play out in my mind when my life gets unpredictable—the common triggers being death, divorce, injury, unemployment, betrayal, and so on. Here is the key point: none of these predictions came true either.

It dawned on me that I had wasted a ton of mind energy inventing these horrible scenarios of my future because clearly, I had proven that I was, in fact, super-sucky at predicting my future. Therefore, I decided to start learning to pull myself back in and focus on right now instead.

I simply cannot know what tomorrow holds—period. Every tomorrow I have ever imagined has been different from what I either expected or planned. Some better, some worse, but never like expected. So it no longer makes sense to me to let my mind scare the shit out of me so much.

I've learned to bring myself back to right now by imagining those hairs that stand up straight because of static electricity. Each hair is one of my tiny thought pieces, worries, memories, to-do list items, fantasies; anywhere my mind happens to go is one of those floating static-filled hairs. I take a deep breath and imagine attracting all those strands back into me wherever I'm standing or sitting. I do this a lot when I'm washing dishes, folding laundry, getting ready for bed, or whenever I start to panic.

I can actually start to feel the energy coming back to me from its crazy worry journey, and I feel stronger and more solid—a bit static electricity-ish but better. Nothing bad is happening to me right *now*. Right *now*, I'm just sitting here. Right *now*, everything is okay. Right *now*, no one is telling me bad news. Right *now*, I hear birds and not a bill collector. Right *now*, my dog is sleeping, and so is my daughter.

Pull the strands back in, and just stay here for a minute because at this moment, you're safe, you're here, and you're fine. Trust me, whatever you are imagining the worst case is or may be, the reality never matches it, so stop imagining what it *could* be like and deal with it later.

Right *now* you are here reading, and that is just fine.

O is for Open

Be open. Be open to trying new things.

That sentence makes me chuckle inside because I don't consider myself particularly adventurous and open to new things anymore, so my suggesting that you should be open to new experiences seems a bit ridiculous and a tad condescending. But I do know it is the correct thing to tell you to do because I need to tell myself to do it too.

For me, if my regular lunch table is already full, and I have to sit somewhere else with new people, I can get a little twitchy and off my game. I guess you could say I like routine maybe a little too much. I don't go out. I don't dress up anymore. I don't travel much. So yes, maybe I'm in a rut that I like to call "my velvet rut" because that is what my dad's sister, Aunt Jo, called it once.

I have been closed for a long time now. Probably due to the lack of some of the twenty-six items in this book. Lack of faith closes me up. Loss of trust closes me up. Feeling unloved closes me up. My choice to close up shop feels like the safe choice, but it is really making no choice at all, which, of course, is a choice. Doing nothing is still a choice. I am not put in the position of experiencing anything when I hide. Nothing new is presented, nothing challenges me, and nothing intrigues me, excites me, or energizes me. Being closed is not a quality choice because it is lame when I consider a moment of frustration or annoyance as adding a spark to my day.

I have a million excuses for why I don't go out, dress up, or talk to people anymore, but no more excuses. For one day I can be open. It's a single day, right? Here we go. I have made a terrifying list.

I will be open to new ideas.
I will be open to listening to different opinions.
I will be open to crazy ideas, like eating out (gasp).
I will be open to trying something new.
I will be open to accepting help.
I will be open to trusting others.
I will be open to the idea that I matter.
I will be open to not knowing what my next step will be.
I will be open to new friends.
I will be open to new places.
I will be open to new ways of thinking.
I will be open to a little discomfort in order to better explore the world around me.

I think it has been a long time since I've opened myself up to others because being closed off feels safer and more comfortable. It's spring, so I should be opening the doors and windows inside and outside of me, and letting the fresh new breezes blow through. And if you're listening, breeze, feel free to take all the dog and cat hair with you. Thanks.

Grab a pencil and paper, and start to make your own terrifying list of phrases that start with, "I will be open to." Just keep going until you stop. I was amazed at some of the things that came through me on to my list, and it feels less scary now because I am also open to learning new things about myself.

Good luck!

P is for Pray

We are more than halfway through *26 Days to Practice Peace*, and I'm here to say that the word "pray" gives me the willies.

I am hopeful you will stay with me, though, because hopefully, I've earned some of your trust.

When I was little, I said my prayers before bed, and I imagined God up in heaven listening to me, smiling through his long white beard and wearing his soft white robe. In fact, God and Santa had very similar faces in my childhood mind.

As the years passed, my connection to religion faded. But my commitment to being a better person expanded. I have committed myself to kindness, compassion, honesty, love, forgiveness, and most important for me is my commitment to refraining from being judgmental and critical of others. I have not quite mastered not judging or criticizing myself yet, but I'll get there. It's easier to be kind to others than to be kind to myself, considering my struggle with love of oneself.

Back to why "pray" give me the willies. I feel nervous in churches—so many rules, procedures, traditions, and protocols. You would think a rule follower like me would love that, but I don't. The perfectionist in me is always worried I will screw it up some way, embarrass myself or others, make everyone turn and stare, offend the old woman next to me, or worse—piss off God in some way.

I also get twitchy when people say they will pray for me. Maybe at some point in my youth I was confronted by some eager Christian praying over me so forcefully that it frightened me. I have no actual memory of this, but I'm certain my self-conscious inner child knew she was being judged harshly. So I continue to hang on to a stubborn refusal to "be prayed for." My insides say, "Don't. I don't need it. Move along. Nothing to see here." I continue to feel weird having people pray for me. It makes me feel like they're judging me and have decided that I'm so screwed up and Godless that they had better get some help for me fast, before the earth cracks open and takes me down to hell.

Clearly, I have some issues. I can see it all unfolding here as I write.

But I do pray—in a way—my way. I talk to "God," I guess you could say. It's hard for a pragmatic spiritualist like me to say I'm talking to God. I would need some sort of proof or memo "From the desk of God" to know for sure whom I'm talking to, but I do believe there is a universal life force that vibrates through everything. So I guess that's who or what I talk to but "God" for short works for me.

When I pray, I complain, I cry, I wish, I yell. But I also send love off to anywhere and anyone I think might want it. At other times, I pray for strength, I pray for money, I pray for good health, I pray for my daughter to have a great day, and I pray for anyone blowing out birthday candles that his or her future is happy and healthy. I prayed that my big dog would live a lot longer, and then I prayed that he would die without pain. I pray my little dog stops waking me at 2:30 a.m. to go out, but then I suck it up, roll out of bed, and realize that now I have to thank God that she *does* wake me up so I have fewer pee spots on my floor.

I guess I pray a lot, but I won't tell you that "I'm praying for you." I will say, "I'm thinking of you." I won't say, "You're in my prayers." I'll say, "You're in my thoughts." Where my fear of prayer came from, I'm not sure, and I don't really care. I'm certain God, the Universe, Spirit, or whatever understands and doesn't really care either.

So for each of you, just know that I'm thinking of you, and I wish you love, light, clarity, peace, and joy. And now you know exactly what I mean. It's sincere and honest and comes from my heart.

What do your prayers look like? What can you pray for today? How will that look and sound? It's a single day to pray, and whatever you decide to call it, the result is more love in the world, so we all win.

Q is for Quiet

In the not so distant past, when I was busy being a stay-at-home/work-from-home mom, I noticed a shift as I was working, but not really succeeding, in my business endeavor. I noticed that I would get nervous as Sunday would end and Monday would begin.

All the noise and activity from the weekend ended as I sent my daughter off to school and closed the back door. The peace and quiet I had wished for mid-Saturday had finally arrived, and because I'm an introvert, I desperately needed this time because I wanted to be reenergized by some good, old-fashioned alone time. But during that year, Monday mornings started to feel different to me. The house was so quiet it hurt my ears. Really. The silence was so loud it seemed to echo noiselessness in my head. That was a little scary. I had never been afraid of the quiet before. I had never dreaded alone time before. What was happening?

I had to make friends with this new quiet, or I was certain I would go crazy. Some people love to turn on music or the television to drown out the silence, but I really do appreciate the quiet. I love it when it's quiet, but it had started to feel very different, and I found myself running to turn on the television to avoid dealing with the constant noise of my quiet.

I think my new quiet was holding a mirror to me and my life. I had to face some pretty big truths about my life. The biggest one was the fact that I was hiding. I had been hiding from admitting that I needed to make some major changes in my business and my life. I was hiding from the truth that I wanted to be writing, but I wasn't writing. I was hiding from the truth that I was angry about several things that recently occurred instead of admitting I was just plain pissed about betrayal and loss. I was "behaving." And I was putting on a forgiving face for others to see. I was hiding from the truth that I needed help but was afraid to reach out to friends for fear of refusal.

This new quiet was so damn loud that there were moments when I would walk through the house and scream to drown it out as I moved from task to task. Finally, I started to talk to it, asking it what the hell it wanted from me. There were moments of self-loathing that I had to get through in order to find out all the things in my life I had been hiding from. And thanks to this quiet, I realized that I was not going to be able to hide anymore.

I had made it my friend. It helped me start writing again, it kept me company while job hunting, it supported me through some self-exploration, and I'm happy to say that my quiet time is once again quiet. My entire life I have never been afraid of silence and didn't understand other people's need to fill the void. I now know the fear that comes with silence. It is scary.

If today is to be a successful day of quiet, you will need to turn off the car radio, Bluetooth, phone and computer notifications, and any other noisy distractions. This isn't the same as a day of silence; you can still talk to people and have conversations. It is just that during car rides, bus rides, walks outside, any alone time, there are to be no earbuds, music, television, YouTube videos, and so on. My only advice here is that silence is not fatal. The fear you feel during the quiet is perhaps trying to teach you something. If you take the leap of faith to talk to the quiet, I'm sure there are lessons there for you too. Try to take the whole day without the music and television. If there is anything the quiet is trying to tell you, trust me, you won't have to work at it. If your quiet wants you to know something, it will be crazy loud!

R is for Respect

One of the three definitions of respect in the *Concise Oxford English Dictionary* is, "due regard for the feelings or rights of others." This is the respect I am offering today.

The primary definition (if they are written in a hierarchy) typically focuses on admiration based a person's qualities or achievements. But this is not where I place my attention today. I don't need to be impressed; I want to extend to you the respect you deserve regardless. I think too many people would be neglected if I waited for them to impress me with some random particular quality or achievement of my inner design that they had no clue I was waiting on.

I prefer to extend respect to others regardless of whether I agree with them or even know anything about them. The feelings and rights of others, a person's right to maintain an opinion contradictory to my own, I respect that. I respect a person willing to disagree with me politely. I don't like confrontation. I enjoy civil discourse, and I love a good debate. What I don't love is another person's refusal to let me speak my piece. When this happens I will, however, respect the fact that someone has different feelings, opinions, behaviors, or social protocols than me, and then I will remove myself from the unpleasant interaction.

Because I respect both you and me means I don't need to continue to interact with you if I am no longer enjoying the interaction. Disagreeing with you doesn't imply a lack of respect. Any behavior toward you that is mean, hurtful, malicious, or spiteful would demonstrate a lack of respect for your existence, and this is the kind of behavior I avoid because it causes me physical pain to witness these types of interactions.

Lately, I have had many interactions that felt either confrontational toward me or, my biggest pet peeve, felt as if I am completely disregarded as being present in the room or conversation. I'm not a big fan of these feelings, but I realize they have something to teach me about how I interact with others. I am capable of inserting myself into situations, or deescalating confrontation for the most part, but those aren't my growth areas. The growth area for me is improving my ability to walk away. If I am completely honest with myself, I have stayed in situations and relationships far beyond their expiration dates. I have taken to extending my regard for another far longer than I should have in order to avoid conflict with or hurting someone else. This has ended up hurting me and completely disregarded the act of being respectful of my own feelings and rights.

I have asked myself, "Why am I working so hard to be gentle of another's feelings at the expense of my own, especially when the other person has paid very little attention to mine?" The first time I asked myself this I was fifty-two years old. That is many, many cumulative years of not extending myself the respect I have given others.

I do believe you get what you give, but I also believe it is possible to give out so much in a certain way that it almost refuses to welcome anything back. I've heard myself saying, "I give and I give so much! When is it my turn?" The bitter pill it took me fifty-two years to swallow was that it was never going to be my turn because I didn't respect myself enough to ask for what I needed or to say no. I didn't respect myself enough to walk away from a disagreement, from disrespectful treatment, from rude or selfish behavior, or from any form of bullshit that didn't align with who I am. Walking away doesn't have to be permanent. It can be simply leaving a room before I say something I regret, or as it has taken me a while to learn, just asking for what I need in a clear, direct way.

Respect today will have you trying this: I offer up my respect for the day to all the people, places, plants, and animals that I encounter, and that includes me. In order to feel less ignored, I will work on not ignoring others. I will work on listening to opposing points of view in order to help mine be heard. I will work on asking for things that

I need, whether it's help, attention, a shoulder to cry on, or a pep talk to get me through the day. I do this for others, and instead of wondering when it will be my turn, I will keep improving my self-respect by asking for what I need. You should to.

S is for Service

A twenty-four-hour period to be of service to anything and anyone in need is where today will take us. Look around to see where you can lend a hand. It's true that helping others is really helping ourselves. Whether or not I get acknowledged for providing a little extra help has become completely unnecessary. I admit I used to want a little bit of praise for how wonderful I was to do this or do that for you, but the more help I gave, the less I wanted any attention. I grew out of it, I guess you could say.

It's easier than you think to find little ways to be of service. Exploring the extra things around you that need help getting finished might lead to exploring the larger things around you where you can lend a hand. For example, picking up bits of paper as you walk the halls at work, throwing away the trash you find walking from point A to point B. Sweeping the sidewalk works, as does mowing the side yard shared with a neighbor, holding the door open for someone, or letting a frazzled-looking person ahead of you in line.

Finding simple things that might impact someone else's day are great acts of service to start with. Finding the time within your life to take part in larger service projects—like neighborhood cleanup, food banks, or animal shelters—can seem overwhelming because of how busy your life feels. Finding the elusive extra time starts with finding the small bits of time within your current routine to start small.

Keep a box in your trunk. Pick up a few extra things at the store when you're shopping, and put them into the box. You never have to carry them into the house, and when the box is full, you can take it to a food bank or church. I shop every weekend. One extra pair of socks, toothpaste, whatever is buy one get one free will essentially add up to fifty-two things a year to donate, minimum. Likely, it will be more because there may be a great deal on some nonperishable food items, but my math doesn't lie; fifty-two donated items is greater than zero donated items.

Keep a box in your closet or under a desk. Search your belongings for things that sit and stare at you unused and longing to be useful to someone else. I mean, how many sets of earbuds does any one person need? This box requires a bit more motivation to get outside the house. My box or bag typically spends a few weeks at the top of the stairs, then a few more weeks by the back door, and then another couple weeks in my trunk (next to the shopping extras box). It really doesn't matter if the box of items spends a month in your trunk. It will get to where it belongs eventually. Mine always has.

Return to the list you compiled in the "G Is for Generosity" chapter. What are some organizations or ideas from this list that you can research today? What sorts of things do the organizations need? Is there a box you can start filling today? Newspapers for the dog shelter, extra blankets for a homeless shelter, or bottled water and school supplies for a teacher you know?

Today is our day of service, so for the day, we really can just start making our plans. We can't accomplish it all, but we can get our boxes ready, we can research our generosity list, and we can extend a helping hand to people who cross our paths today.

You never have to leap into the deep end first thing if you don't want to. Being of service to others becomes a habit if you start small and introduce yourself to the little things you can actually see through to the end. Remember that just because it's a small act of service doesn't mean it isn't filling a giant need for someone else.

T is for Trust

The idea for *26 Days to Practice Peace* came to me a few years after a list of twenty-six words flew through my fingertips on to a page in my notebook. I thought, *What a great idea to create something for people to work their way through for twenty-six days.* My hope was that at the end of those days, there would be a subtle shift in your life from one place—maybe isolation, maybe stagnation, maybe a scattered feeling—to a place of comfort, focus, and confidence.

I made that list of twenty-six words in a matter of moments, not really thinking about them at all, just satisfying my curiosity about matching the alphabet with my life philosophy. Then the list sat and sat and sat for months. I never changed any of the words corresponding to its letter. I felt like the word that popped up for me at the time was a word that I needed to spend a day with in order to get to know it and understand why it came to me on the list.

What would I choose as the scariest word on the list? Trust. Trust is one of those words that needs some serious work on my part.

After a lot of disappointments, struggling to control everything, and failure, I have given up the need to demand control of my life and the direction it's taking. I tell myself that I trust the universe to point me in the right direction to learn all that I need to learn. I just need to consistently show up each day dedicated to being the best version of myself, take what life offers, learn the lessons presented, and keep the faith, so to speak.

Trusting the universe is a piece of cake for me. Trusting my fellow human beings is where I struggle.

Like everyone I'm sure, I've been let down by the people I know, the people I love, the people I trust. My problem is that after a few letdowns, I have chosen to withdraw and stop investing myself in trusting others. When people say they will do something for me, my typical reply is, "No thanks. That's not necessary." Why do I do that? Because over the years, the people I loved and depended on to deliver on their promises did not. It occurred to me that it was safer to stop asking for or accepting things—like help—because if I never asked or accepted, I could never feel disappointed by others.

A small example of this is a story I tell to demonstrate that letdown feeling. It happened about twenty-five years ago, around Valentine's Day. I was asked by my significant other (at the time) what I wanted for Valentine's Day. I said that if he really wanted to do anything at all for me, it would be to take the dogs to get groomed. Not very romantic on my part, but it was a luxury I wanted to give both my dogs and me because then I wouldn't have to bathe them. I reiterated how desperately I wanted this; I said I didn't want any Victoria's Secret (the typical gift), and if he really wanted to be my hero, he would take the dogs to the groomers for me. When I got home from work on February 14, I found two lovely pink boxes from Victoria's Secret on my bed.

These types of events started to show me a pattern of me asking for A and getting B in return. Therefore, I ultimately stopped asking because I didn't trust people anymore. This is a dangerous place to live, not trusting others. My dogs/undergarment example is not a huge betrayal or letdown in the grand scheme of things, but my loss of trust in others is a result of a series of these tiny events, along with more traumatic ones that have made me perhaps a little too stubborn and resistant to seek help or kindness from others.

I have decided to use this day to trust that the lessons I need to learn will present themselves to me in ways that I can understand and resolve with very little pain. I will work on learning to take people at their word and, more important, to *not* feel as though I am somehow to blame if they don't follow through. To *not* determine I wasn't worthy of their follow-through if they were unable to deliver. To stop assuming that just because I may ask for a certain type of help in the form of A that perhaps B can't be useful too.

It is okay to ask for help and to trust the people in your life. But if other people do not behave in ways that we expect them to, well, duh, that's not really realistic in the first place, is it? The only person I can control is me; I need to reenter the world of trusting my fellow humans and letting go of my expectations.

Let's enter our day with a sense of trust that things will go exactly as they should, and if someone offers something for us, we will trust that he or she means it.

U is for Universe

I remember once when I was about eight, I lay across my bed on my back, my head hanging over the side, and looking out my window. The clouds were moving slowly. The longer I lay there and watched the clouds, the more I felt as if I was the one moving, not the clouds. I felt as if I could feel the spin of the earth through my body. Suddenly, I felt very small but strangely powerful there, able to hang on to my bed and not fly off.

In the past year, I have tried to have this experience again; I have failed. Thankfully though, I have it in my imagination. I can see my old bedroom, the window, the clouds upside down. I just can't feel the spinning anymore.

Today I think I will place all my worries, fears, and insecurities in a box under the childhood bed in my mind, and remember how big the universe really is and how small the items in my box are. In comparison, my lifetime is a blink, and today is even shorter. So setting aside all that frightens me for one day to simply sit back and enjoy the wonder of the universe will be okay. I will be fine. You will too.

Today I will look closely at the things coming to life in my yard, and I will listen closely to the birds singing outside my windows. I will watch my daughter when she isn't looking, and I will sit outside in the sun with my dog. I will lie on the trampoline that swallows my yard and is a pain in the ass to mow around, and I will stare at the clouds and then at the moon as the day ends.

I have a tiny backyard that overlooks an alley. My neighborhood is old, and my life is modest and small. When I compare myself to others, I can feel "less"—less successful, less affluent, less attractive, less intelligent, less, less, less. When I compare my worries to the universe, I realize how none of that stuff matters. Then I realize I live in a magical place that contains so many things deserving of appreciation that I can stand to take a day off from my worries and appreciate how big and wonderful my universe really is.

Take time today to pack up the box with your worries, fears, and insecurities. Shove it under the bed. Enjoy your universe. Look around and feel the spinning with you and all you have to appreciate at its center.

V is for Vision

My vision for my future is in deep, deep transition. In fact, I think it would be very cool if I could receive a vision of my future, my life, my anything just to give me a hint of which way I should go.

I believe it's important to have a general hope for the future, a loose road map for life. My problem has been that I set those expectations of how it should go, and then I become far too attached to the outcome. Most of the time the attachment to "my way" and the expectation of "should be" has led to deep disappointment in myself and my fellow humans. Shame and blame, what an awful partnership. That duo has visited me so much that I'm choosing to set a course for a future that I have absolutely no idea where I'm heading.

I have my priorities: food, shelter, healthy and safe child, healthy father, healthy pets, happy home, and comfy clothes. But I have lost my vision for my future. Nothing so far turned out as expected for me, which is not a crime. It really isn't even horrible. I am content. But it has made me rethink my vision for the future. My old visions were filled with accomplishments, accolades, and material goods. The fact that I have survived on much less has forced me to reconsider the value of those visions.

My new vision for the future is to be happy. Be happy—that's it. I've learned that I am completely capable of doing many jobs, leading many people, organizing many projects, and solving many problems in very different settings over the past thirty-five years, and what matters most to me is the happiness I bring with me while doing these things. Sharing my happy with others and seeing them happy have been enough lately. I don't think that will change.

Laughter has returned to my world, along with an appreciation of the smallest of things. Worry has subsided, and my all-time constant companion, fear, has been shown the door. Yes, there are still moments of worry and fear, but I am much better these days at holding an accurate view of what realistic worry/fear is as opposed to what totally over the top, outta my mind, stupid worry/fear is. This is a major achievement for me and my life. I attribute it to my new and improved vision for life—happiness.

W is for ~~Wisdom~~
Willingness

When I wrote "T Is for Trust," I explained where my list of words came from and the feeling of pride in the fact that I hadn't changed a single word over the years. Until now. I think it's appropriate that my W word became "willingness" because I needed to learn how to be willing to be flexible when it came to changing my mind and my word.

I was having trouble writing for wisdom. I had an idea of what I wanted to share, but it just wasn't working. I was discussing my list and my W woes with one of my new coworkers and friend. He asked me, "Does it have to be wisdom?"

"Well, I wrote down my list of words months and months ago, and I've never changed one, not once. But I guess it doesn't *have* to be." I could feel myself getting all bristly and defensive at the thought of changing a word—*my* word. I had been so prideful of my list, assuming each word had something wonderful to teach me.

"How about willingness?" he asked.

Ding, ding, ding, we have a winner. I knew he was right the moment he said it, but I felt a tiny sting of interior resistance about changing my word. It was a fast realignment inside, and I realized that I had to be willing to change.

Duh.

Maybe this was wisdom's lesson for me after all. Stop being so damn rigid. Let others in, let someone else help, and for Pete's sake, be willing to do all the above.

So keyboard and virtual paper in hand, I made a list of willingness with my top fear as the first one.

I will be willing to fail.
I will be willing to succeed.
I will be willing to meet new people.
I will be willing to take advice.
I will be willing to listen to opposing points of view.
I will be willing to change my opinions after getting new
    information.
I will be willing to smile.
I will be willing to play outside.
I will be willing to go out to dinner.
I will be willing to wear makeup for no reason.
I will be willing to try to put an effort into my appearance.
I will be willing to eat more veggies.
I will be willing to drink less wine.

I will be willing not to feel as if the world will end if I spend money on a treat for me or my daughter.
I will be willing to get rid of some things.
I will be willing to be less afraid.
I will be willing to be less critical of myself.
I will be willing to love me.
I will be willing to listen to criticism without feeling pain.
I will be willing to dust myself off and try again.

Willingness is the key to having any new experiences at all or to making any changes in the way things are going. I can feel it in my belly when I'm unwilling. Sometimes that's a good thing; my belly is my sensory warning that I need to pay attention. Other times it is just regular run-of-the-mill fear trying to keep me in my velvet rut.

Fear knows that getting out of any rut requires a change, perhaps a new me with new friends and new ways of seeing the world. That might make my old friends very uncomfortable, but I am not responsible for how they feel about me. That's a tough one to get past, especially when I don't really consider myself as having many friends to spare. If you look at my list, you can probably tell my nature keeps me out of the crowds.

I am both excited and frightened by my list, and I need to take some time with each of them. To get enough traction to start getting out of any rut begin using the phrase, "I'm willing to consider that," and then see where it takes you.

Being willing to change even the smallest thing could ripple into so much more as we open up and explore new things. What are the things you might put on your list? Are you willing to put pen to paper today to come up with an equally frightening list? I hope you do, and I hope you're willing to share that list with me and others.

X is for Xanadu

The perfect place.

The word "perfect" doesn't scare me. Using it doesn't set me up for unrealistic expectations even with my perfectionist tendencies. I think it scares other people when I use the word more than it does me. People like to fire back at me with a quick reminder of "nothing's perfect" or "perfection is overrated" as a way to comfort me when I use the word. I think they're comforting themselves, or reminding themselves in some small way to not set the bar too high. I don't need that protection, and I'm also not completely sure that I agree that "nothing's perfect." Nature holds many perfections: a flower, a beehive, a tree, even a tornado.

I learned an exercise a few years ago to help me feel better. I close my eyes and try to experience how it would feel if everything in my life were perfect. And yes, that is the word that was used: "perfect."

It's a surprisingly relaxing and easy thing to do to imagine how perfect feels. The key is the *feeling* of perfection, not the *seeing* of perfection. The feeling of perfection takes my mind off the items that are distracting or disturbing me. If I'm busy imagining how I would *feel* if all things were perfect, it's impossible for me to cling to the worries that float around my mind.

I did this for a few days very consistently, until I didn't. I stopped. Life got in the way—shitty to be exact—and I neglected my perfect. One morning after I sent my daughter off to school, the silence of the house and my life screamed at me the way it enjoyed doing. I was busy beating myself up for being taken advantage of, humiliated, betrayed— take your pick—it all happened. Then I remembered "perfection." I decided to sit and *feel* perfection for a while.

I sat down, closed my eyes, and let out a big sigh. As I sat there, imagining the feeling of a perfect life, I had an epiphany. The perfection I was feeling was the way I felt about my life *in that very moment.* I *was* living a perfect life. My eyes popped open, and I was smiling. *My life is perfect right now,* I thought. Wow.

Perfection was a feeling, not the tiny house I rented, the temporary feelings of sadness I had, or the balance in my bank account. It wasn't the weather, the city where I live, the chipped china plates, nail polish stains in the sink, broken floor tiles, or muddy dog prints on my floor. I was in the middle of having a perfect life, and it felt like peace.

The circumstances we find ourselves in will come and go—endlessly. Waiting for the perfect life isn't necessary at all. It took me a while, but I get it. It's not a place. It's a feeling, and if we can tap into that feeling every now and again to remind ourselves, we get to experience the perfection of our life right now. We get to set down the hurt, anger, and disappointment and realize how great we have it right now—chipped plates, filthy house, muddy pets, and all.

Y is for Youthful

When I was in my twenties, basking in the youthful glow of being, well, twenty, I gave my mother a birthday card with a quote attributed to Mark Twain in it. Something along the lines of age being a matter of mind: "If you don't mind, it doesn't matter." At that time, my mom was nearing fifty, and I am certain my naïve attitude toward aging was that it just shouldn't be that big of a deal. My mother felt differently. Aging was difficult for her emotionally, and the saddest part is she never got to actually experience it. She died at fifty-nine. And while I joke that she clearly was prepared to do *anything* to not turn sixty, she and I missed a lot of time together.

I don't know how it felt to her on her landmark birthdays, like forty or fifty, but I know she was grumpy when she turned forty because my father warned me and my brother to steer clear. I was thirteen at the time and far too self-absorbed in my middle-school angst to really care, so I just steered clear.

All I know now, at age fifty-four is that I don't *feel* fifty-four. I feel like I'm so much younger in my head. As long as I don't see my reflection, I can feel like I'm twenty but with the wisdom of fifty. I think our emotional, inner age only needs to match our chronological age if we make that choice, and I have *not* made that choice. Yes, I have aches and pains, and I have a wider waistband than I used to. But my attitude on most days can be considered youthful and bright.

I attribute my youthful attitude to the fact that I spent twenty-three years around ten- to eighteen-year-olds, trying to get them to love math by making an ass out of myself. But that may or may not be the direct source. It could be a chicken-or-the-egg kind of relationship. Perhaps it's that my inner goofiness and childlike qualities made me perfect to teach math. Notice I said childlike, not childish. I just wanted to put that out there.

It could also be genetics. My father, at age ninety-one, doesn't feel ninety-one until something that used to be very easy for him has become difficult enough to require him to sit and catch his breath. He told me, "Of course, I always feel like I'm twelve," and I believe him. He is a very youthful ninety-one-year-old. He only seems old when he's sad. I see and hear it when he tells me about a death among his contemporaries, and they might be as many as twenty years younger than him. Most people who meet him are shocked to learn his age.

Like Dad, my interior youthful feeling doesn't always match my exterior abilities, like how my body reacts to jumping on the trampoline with my daughter. I don't think that's age, though. I think it's my lack of exercise catching up with me. But what if it isn't? What if I'm kidding myself, and I really am getting old? Nope, not today. I'm still not making that choice.

Being youthful for a day requires some adjustments. Try not spending a lot of time in front of a mirror. This helps me maintain the illusion of my youth. I'm fascinated with the phenomenon of how young I feel—inside. When I do catch sight of me in a mirror, I am almost always taken aback by my appearance. I see my mother looking at me, which isn't a bad thing; it's just a shocking thing. I'm not expecting her to show up in the mirror. I'm expecting to see the version of me I see in my head.

Play also needs to make its way into your day. Laughing and acting silly are almost must-dos. If you take yourself too seriously every single day, I predict some premature aging heading your way. I enjoy being goofy, laughing, and just plain acting silly. It's a great stress reliever.

You also need to goof off a bit today. I have decided it's true, but I don't know who said, "Youth is wasted on the young." There are days when I can feel the childlike ornery rise up inside me, and I just want to push someone's shit off the edge of anything, just like cats do. I want to laugh until I nearly pee my pants, not because I'm losing bladder control, but because whatever it is was so damn funny. I want to ring a doorbell and run away, but I can't; I'm too slow now. But there are things that can bring back a taste of youth. Find yours and do it, think about it, imagine it, and let your inner you feel young again.

This isn't about age-defying formulas for the skin, fewer wrinkles, or living forever. It's about the enjoyment of feeling youthful and not taking everything so damn seriously. This is the key anti-aging formula to bring to your beauty routine. We just need to remember to apply it every day.

Z is for Zest

Now that you know me better, it may seem like the obvious choice for Z would have been zen, but my mind always returns to a family tradition that began around 1975. For Christmas I was given a gift from my grandmother wrapped in this red holiday alphabet paper: A is for angel, B is for bedtime, all the way to Z is for zestful. A cute picture of a boy holding flowers in one hand with the other outstretched, like he was singing while standing on a little soapbox. I memorized that list that year and had my parents quiz me constantly. So yes, it is completely confirmed at the end of the alphabet that I have always been a wordy nerd. I recited the list so many times that year, waiting to unwrap my gift Christmas morning, that my mom, dad, and brother also knew the entire list: R is for rocking horse, S is for stocking.

My dad saved that paper as he often did, having been a Depression-era child, and it became a Christmas tradition when the decorations came out to see who could remember all the letters. We would work our way through it collectively before the paper was found. My mom used to enjoy this the most. I can still remember her being the first one as the holiday approached to start the list, "A is for angel," she'd begin. "Let's see, B is for boxes?" It was our family game. I was probably destined to create a list from A to Z that would fit my life and my way of seeing the world.

Over the years, the paper started to tear, so my dad, able to find three complete A to Z panels, had them framed. One for me, another for my brother, and the last one for himself to remind him of my mother and the game, I'm sure. It was always a grand accomplishment—worthy of a toast—if we could all collectively get to Z is for zestful without any cheating and peeking at the paper.

The best part of having my framed wrapping paper is, although my mom died over twenty years ago, I can still hear her voice prompting us all, "Let's see, A is for angel," and laughing as we all competed to see who came up with the next letter/word combo the fastest—with zest you might say.

It's important to find the pieces of your life that can be filled with the fervor and gusto of great joy. Throwing your chest out and arms open wide as if to sing like the little zestful boy on my wrapping paper!

Too often in life we move from point A to point B because it was on our checklist of accomplishments, duties, obligations, or responsibilities. And the little moments to relish of glee, passion, laughter, and fun get missed, or worse, simply set aside and overlooked in the name of completion. In life there is no straight line from point A to point B, and passing up the moments in order to get there faster is a waste of some solid joy and laughter.

Make a choice. One moment of zest per day. Wake with vigor, stretch out your arms wide, breathe in deeply, and twist like a sprinkler. Breathe out a long, heavy, noisy sigh. Startle the cat, the dog, or the neighbor. Laugh. Sing loudly in the car on your way to your next destination, and look over to find someone staring at you. Laugh. Look in the mirror and smile until you feel foolish. Laugh. Talk to your food, your pets, your furniture. Give them speeches about the qualities they possess that make you happy. Laugh. Narrate your day as you fold the laundry or sort the mail, as if anyone listening cares. Do it until you feel foolish. Laugh.

I talk to myself a lot as I wander around the house doing chores. "Up the stairs, down the stairs," I say as I make my trips. I hear my daughter ask, "Mom, are you okay?" And I say, "Yes, just talking to myself." She laughs, and so do I. It's about the joy I infuse into the tiny tasks I have to complete. It's about the laughter that happens between getting my chores done and fulfilling my obligations that gives me joy.

So here's a toast to me and you, to family, friends, fun, and memories for making it from A to Z with me on our journey. I'm feeling a bit zestful having made a new friend, knowing that you are here at Z with me on these pages. My wish for us both is that each time we think about working through A to Z, we learn even more about ourselves each time. I remain convinced that I can pretty much participate in anything for just a day as long as I'm open to "trying without crying."

Thank you for being here with me.

Twenty-Six Days Checklist

Read. Reflect. Resolve.

Day	Was the day easy?			Thoughts about the day. Am I good at this? Potential for change?
	Yes	No	Meh	
Accept				
Breathe				
Compassion				
Divinity				
Epiphany				
Faith				
Generosity				
Heart				
Imagination				
Joy				

Kindness				
Love				
Meditate				
Now				
Open				
Pray				
Quiet				
Respect				
Service				
Trust				
Universe				
Vision				
Willingness				
Xanadu				
Youthful				
Zest				

When all twenty-six days are finished, take a day or two away from your list.

Celebrate every easy day as one of your strengths. These strengths easily live within you and are there for you to lean on when you chose to work on a day that didn't go well. The days that didn't go well are likely areas of ourselves we can easily see as ones to improve, and starting with one of these can be a great choice.

The meh days are ones to really ponder. These may be areas that are so hidden from our view we may not want to face them. If you get that feeling about a day, you may not be ready yet. If you're super brave, you can ask someone close to you for input. "Do I seem unforgiving?" or, "Do I come across as stingy, self-centered, flighty, or rigid?" As always, if something seems too hard to face right now, then wait. I can almost promise it will show itself again at some point, and when it does, maybe that time you'll be ready to see it.

Choose something that looks like an easy thing to face first, and resolve to do better, be better. The universe always has a way of showing us these things again and again. My areas to improve list can change month to month. I will face things, do some hard work, do better, have record breaking growth, and then, sure enough, life gets in the way. Something happens, I label it "bad," and I hide from facing my growth all over again.

Welcome to being a human. It's something we all have in common. You are capable, and you are enough.

Printed in the United States
By Bookmasters